DINOSAURS AND THEIR DISCOVERERS™

Ichthyosaurus and Little Mary Anning

Brooke Hartzog

The Rosen Publishing Group's
PowerKids Press™
New York

Published in 1999 by The Rosen Publishing Group, Inc.
29 East 21st Street, New York, NY 10010

First Edition

Book Design: Danielle Primiceri

Photo Credits: pp. 4, 6, 21 © American Museum of Natural History; pp. 5, 18, 22 © Jonathan Blair/Corbis; pp. 9, 14 © 1997 Digital Vision Ltd., p. 10 © Simon Battensby/Tony Stone Images; p. 13 © 1996 PhotoDisc Inc.; p. 17 © Life around Jurassic shores, 165 million years ago by English School (20th century) Natural History Museum, London, UK/Bridgeman Art Library, London/New York.

Hartzog, Brooke.
    Ichthyosaurus and little Mary Anning / by Brooke Hartzog.
            p.   cm. — (Dinosaurs and their discoverers)
    Includes index.
    Summary: An account of the English girl who, at age twelve, discovered the first complete ichthyosaurus skeleton, and who continued to collect and study dinosaur fossils throughout her life.
    ISBN 0-8239-5326-2
    1. Anning, Mary, 1799–1847—Juvenile literature. 2. Women paleontologists—England—Biography—Juvenile literature. 3. Ichthyosaurus—Juvenile literature. [1. Anning, Mary, 1799–1847. 2. Paleontologists. 3. Women—Biography.] I. Title. II. Series: Hartzog, Brooke. Dinosaurs and their discoverers.
QE707/A56H37 1998
560'.92—dc21   98-10339
[B]   CIP
                                                                        AC

Manufactured in the United States of America

Contents

Little Girl Discoverer

There is a place near the seashore in England called Lyme Regis. In 1810 a group of scientists gathered there at the home of a little girl named Mary Anning. Mary was about twelve years old. She had found something that many scientists thought was a great discovery.

◄ *Mary Anning was one of the first dinosaur discoverers.*

Mary Anning's discovery of a whole skeleton brought many ► scientists to her town.

She had uncovered the first whole **skeleton** (SKEH-lih-tun) of a dinosaur called an **ichthyosaurus** (IK-thee-uh-SOR-us). Ichthyosaurus means "fishy lizard" in Latin. Scientists called it this because the dinosaur's skeleton looked like a fish and a **reptile** (REP-tyl). The scientists wanted to see Mary's discovery and **examine** (eg-ZA-min) it.

Strange Rocks

Mary's family was very poor. Mary's father, Mr. Anning, was often unable to find work. So he spent time walking along the beaches in Lyme Regis. In the early 1800s, the Lyme Regis beaches were different from other beaches. Most beaches had lots of shells on them. But the beaches in Lyme Regis had many rocks shaped like sea creatures and shells. These rocks were **fossils** (FAH-sulz). Millions of years ago, when plants and animals died, their remains would be covered by layers of **sediment** (SEH-dih-mint). Over time the sediment turned to stone, and the remains of the plants and animals became fossils. Mr. Anning liked to collect these fossils, although he thought they were just strange rocks.

◄ *Fossils are clues to what animal and plant life might have been like in the past.*

Mary Helps Find Fossils

When Mary Anning was old enough, she went to the beaches with her father. Mary helped him collect rocks. At first, no one in the family knew that the strange rocks were fossils. But they did know that they could sell the rocks to people who visited the seashore at Lyme Regis. The Annings collected the rocks, or fossils, in baskets. They took the filled baskets to a busy nearby road. When travelers stopped to rest, Mr. Anning sold the fossils to them.

Here is a rocky seashore that is like the beach where Mary and her father collected fossils. ▶

Mary Becomes a Collector

When Mary was eleven years old, everyone in her family came down with a serious illness. Mary got better. But, sadly, her father died. Mary missed her father very much. So she went to the seashore to collect the fossils by herself. One day she was on her way home with a strange fossil known as an **ammonite** (A-muh-nyt). It looked like a flat snail's shell. Along the way, she met a lady who asked to buy the fossil. With the money in her hand, Mary ran back home with a big smile on her face.

Ammonite fossils have a swirling design and are usually found near seashores.

Mary Helps Her Family

When Mary's father died, her family became even poorer than they were before. Mary's mother was a **widow** (WIH-doh) and couldn't work because she had to take care of Mary's brothers and sisters. Mary decided to collect and sell fossils as often as she could. With the money she made selling fossils to visitors to the seashore, Mary could help her family. Word about Mary's new business spread quickly. People came from near and far to buy her fossils. They even made up a **tongue twister** (TUNG TWIS-ter) about Mary: "She sells seashells by the seashore." Have you heard people try to repeat that tongue twister quickly?

Look carefully at shells when you go to the beach.
You might find a fossil of your own! ▶

Little Girl Scientist

When scientists came to Lyme Regis to **investigate** (in-VES-tih-gayt) the fossils, they often wanted to talk with Mary. Even though she had quit school to help her family earn money, Mary was a very smart girl. And she was better at finding fossils than anyone in Lyme Regis. By speaking with the scientists, Mary discovered that the stones and shells she had been finding were really fossils. Some of them were even parts of dinosaur skeletons.

Visiting scientists often asked Mary to show them around the seashore since she knew so much about it.

Fossils Are Important

    With this new **knowledge** (NAH-lidj), Mary became more excited than ever about searching for fossils. She knew that the strange objects she found were **valuable** (VAL-yoo-bul). They were valuable because she could sell them for more money. They were also valuable because they could help scientists understand more about the past.

    Fossils help scientists figure out what kinds of animals and plants used to live on Earth. Many of those plants and animals are now **extinct** (ik-STINKT).

Fossils are often found in areas that used to be covered by water. Lots of animals came to these areas to drink, and many died nearby. ▶

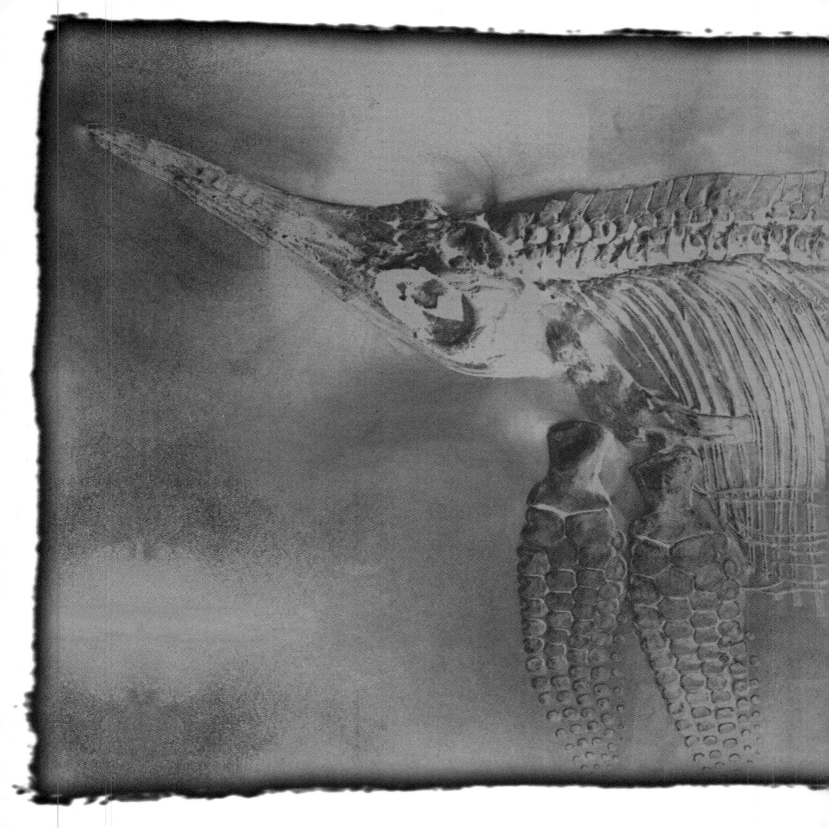

Mary Makes a Discovery

One day, when Mary was twelve, she saw something that looked like a bone sticking out of a rock. Because Mary was learning more and more about fossils, she was sure she had found something very important. Mary carefully used her hammer to chip away the rock around the bone-like object. She discovered that it was just one of many bones that had been buried together millions of years ago. Mary got her brother to help her dig them out of the rock. Soon they saw that they had found a whole skeleton!

◀ *An ichthyosaurus left this skeleton in the earth.*

The First Ichthyosaurus

The **skull** (SKUL) of the skeleton that Mary and her brother dug up looked like a fish head. It had a long snout full of small, sharp teeth. The body was long like a lizard's body. The skeleton also had flippers like a dolphin's. When scientists heard about this exciting discovery, they visited Mary. They told Mary that she was the first person ever to discover a whole skeleton of an ichthyosaurus. This dinosaur lived in an ocean that had covered Lyme Regis millions of years before.

The ichthyosaurus lived millions of years ago, but it looked like some animals that are alive today. ▶

Mary Helps the Scientists

Over time Mary Anning became very famous. Scientists asked for her help with new discoveries. One scientist, William D. Conybeare, had found parts of a dinosaur and he wanted to know more about it. Mary soon found an entire skeleton of that dinosaur and Conybeare named the creature **plesiosaurus** (PLEH-see-uh-sor-us). A plesiosaurus was like an ichthyosaurus because both swam in the ocean. Unlike the ichthyosaurus, though, the plesiosaurus had a very long neck. Mary Anning hunted fossils for the rest of her life. She continued to find hundreds of fossils that helped scientists solve puzzles of the past.

Glossary

ammonite (A-muh-nyt) A mollusk with a flat, spiral shell, or the fossil named after the mollusk.

examine (eg-ZA-min) To look at something carefully in order to learn more about it.

extinct (ik-STINKT) To no longer exist.

fossil (FAH-sul) The hardened remains of a dead animal or plant.

ichthyosaurus (IK-thee-uh-SOR-us) A kind of dinosaur that lived millions of years ago in Earth's oceans.

investigate (in-VES-tih-gayt) To try to learn the facts about something.

knowledge (NAH-lij) Understanding something.

plesiosaurus (PLEH-see-uh-sor-us) A dinosaur that lived in Earth's oceans millions of years ago.

reptile (REP-tyl) A kind of cold-blooded animal, such as a crocodile, a lizard, or a snake.

sediment (SEH-dih-mint) Gravel, sand, silt, or mud that is carried by wind or water.

skeleton (SKEH-lih-tun) The set of all the bones in an animal's body.

skull (SKUL) The bones in an animal's head that protect its brain.

tongue twister (TUNG TWIS-ter) A word or phrase that is difficult to say.

valuable (VAL-yoo-bul) Useful; worth a lot of money.

widow (WIH-doh) A woman whose husband has died.

Index